LEARNING TOGETHER

ADVICE AND INSTRUCTIONS ON COMPLETING THESE TESTS

1. There are 100 questions in each test. Make sure you have not missed a page.

2. Start at question 1 and work your way to question 100.

3. If you are unable to complete a question leave it and go to the next one.

4. Do not think about the question you have just left as this wastes time.

5. If you change an answer make sure the change is clear.

6. Make sure you spell correctly.

7. You may do any rough work on the test paper or on another piece of paper.

8. Each test should take approximately 50 minutes.

9. When you have finished each test mark it with an adult.

10. An adult or parent may be able to explain any questions you do not understand.

TEST 16

SCORE _____

1. Which letter occurs twice in CRENELLATED but once in CREDENTIALS ?   (_____)

2. Which letter occurs once in HARMONIOUS, once in LIBERATE but not at all in MELANCHOLY or in LIKE ?   (_____)

3. Which letter, which occurs more than once, occurs as often in PRIVILEGED as it does in PROCEDURE ?   (_____)

4. Half of a number is three quarters of 12. What is twice that number ?   (_____)

5. Share 360 apples among Paul, Alan and Sam in such a way that for every 3 apples Paul gets, Sam gets 2, and for every 2 apples that Sam gets Alan gets 4. How many apples does Alan get ?   (_____)

In the questions below TWO words must change places so that the sentence makes sense. Underline the TWO words that must change places.

Look at this example: The wood was made of table.

6. Their pupils sat quietly at the desks.

7. In sails fluttered gently the the breeze.

8. Some fins have spiky fish on their backs.

9. David was unable and sick to attend school.

10. Tropical cattle are being cleared to raise forests on the land.

11-15.
**The table below gives some information about the subtraction of numbers in the left hand column from those in the top row.
Complete the table correctly using only the numbers given.**

     5.7,   4.9,   7.3,   7.1,   1.6.

	—	7.8		12.0
11.				
12, 13.		2.9	2.4	
14, 15.		6.2		10.4

In each question below one letter can be removed from the word in the first column and put into the word in the second column to give two new words. The order of the letters is not changed.

Look at this example:
THINS   TOUT   (THIN)   (STOUT)

16. SHOUT   STOP   (_____) (_____)

17. THREAD   SOP   (_____) (_____)

18. HEARD   SET   (_____) (_____)

19. BEAR   OUGHT   (_____) (_____)

20. SPORT   ANTS   (_____) (_____)

TEST 16 PAGE 1.

In each line below write in the brackets one letter which completes the word in front of and the word after the brackets.
Look at this example: ROA (D) OOR

Here D completes ROAD and begins DOOR.

21.   MOS   (____)   IREN

22.   NEX   (____)   APER

23.   PYLO   (____)   AIL

24.   DEPRIV (____)   URASIA

25.   INSER (____)   AN

In each line below underline TWO words, ONE from each side, which together make ONE correctly spelt word. The word on the left always comes first. Look at this example:

<u>BLACK</u> ALL TOP   AND   <u>BIRD</u> BOY

26. ALL   IN   BY   SCORE   SCRIBE   PORT
27. NO   IF   NOW   YES   ON   SO
28. BY   AT   BUTTER   CYCLE   LOST   CUP
29. SAT   UP   SO   BY   URN   GASP
30. PATH   PASS   PART   OLD   PAT   AGE

Write in the brackets a word that rhymes with the second word and has a similar meaning to the first word.

Look at this example: SICK   MILL   (__ILL__)

31. AEROPLANE   MET   (_____)

32. DOG   SOUND   (_____)

33. DISCOVER   LINED   (_____)

In a certain code CHRISTMAS is written as AFPGQRKYQ.
Write the following words in code. The alphabet is printed to help you.

A B C D E F G H I J K L M N O P Q R S T U V W X Y Z

34. BEFORE   (_____)

35. DANGER   (_____)

36. NAPKIN   (_____)

What do these coded words represent?

37. EPMSN   (_____)

38. CKCPEC   (_____)

39. AYJASJYRC   (_____)

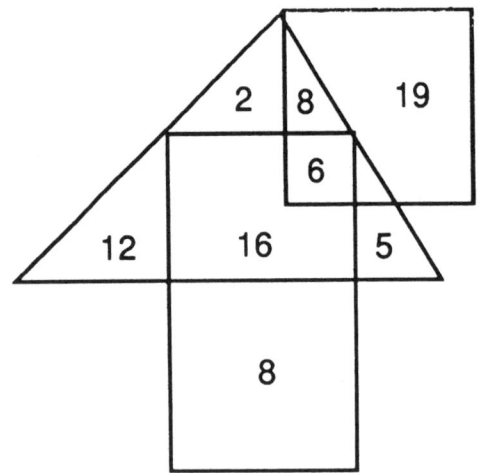

Questions 40-44 are about the above diagram.

40. Which number is in all three shapes ? (_____)

41. From the sum of the numbers appearing only in the square, subtract the sum of the numbers appearing only in the triangle. (_____)

42. What is the sum of all the numbers which appear in more than one shape ? (_____)

43. In how many shapes does the square root of 36 appear ? (_____)

44. Add the two highest even numbers and from the total subtract all the odd numbers. (_____)

6 people U, V, W, X, Y and Z queue for bus tickets at a kiosk window.
Z is not at the rear of the queue and has two people between him and the last person who is not Y. U is not at the rear of the queue and has at least four people ahead of him.
X is not first and is ahead of two people.
W is not first or last in the queue.
List the people in order starting with the person at the front of the queue.

45. (_____) front

46. (_____)

47. (_____)

48. (_____)

49. (_____)

50. (_____) rear

TEST 16 PAGE 3.

Alan, Bob, Carol and Darren take part in a variety of sports.
Only one person takes part in archery and that is not Carol nor Bob.
Bob is the only person taking part in three sports.
Alan takes part in cricket and one other sport.
Darren takes part only in cricket and darts.
Carol takes part only in bowls.

51. Which sport does Bob not take part in ?   (_____)
52. Which person takes part in archery ?   (_____)
53. Who takes part in cricket but not darts ?   (_____)
54. How many people take part in two sports ?   (_____)
55. Who takes part in darts but not bowls ?   (_____)

In questions 56-61 the three words A, B and C are in alphabetical order. The word at B is missing and you are given a dictionary definition instead. Write the correct word in the space.

Look at this example: A) FLAP
                         B) (_ FLARE__) Distress signal from a boat.
                         C) FLASH

56. (A) PREVAIL
    (B) (_____) To stop.
    (C) PREY

57. (A) DUST
    (B) (_____) Of Holland.
    (C) DUTY

58. (A) SCRAP
    (B) (_____) Score with claws or nails.
    (C) SCRAWL

59. (A) MANNER
    (B) (_____) Residence of a minister.
    (C) MANUAL

60. (A) RINSE
    (B) (____) Trouble caused by a crowd of people.
    (C) RIP

61. (A) AKIN
    (B) (____) Mechanical device to arouse people.
    (C) ALBINO

TEST 16 PAGE 4.

The words below and those in the lists are alike in some way. Write the letter of the list, that each word belongs to, in the brackets. Each letter may be used only once.

62. MAJESTIC   (D)
63. GAGGLE   (B)
64. PYRENEES   (C)
65. FORTH   (A)
66. LIME   (E)

A.	B.	C.	D.	E.
MERSEY	SHOAL	ANDES	ELEGANT	BEECH
TYNE	FLOCK	ROCKIES	STATELY	BIRCH
THAMES	LITTER	ALPS	GRACEFUL	OAK

Complete these sequences, the alphabet is printed to help you.

A B C D E F G H I J K L M N O P Q R S T U V W X Y Z

67. A, C, G, M   (U)
68. C, Y, F, V, I   (S)
69. ZYY, ABB, YXX, BCC, XWW   (CDD)
70. ZY, UT, RQ, ML, JI   (ED)

```
              1
              X

    4     3     2
    X     X     X

    5     6
    X     X
```

A, B, C, D, E and F are six towns at the points 1-6 but not in that order.
A is due north of C which is due east of B.
B is due south of F which is one of the two most westerly towns.
E is not furthest north.

71. Which town is at point number 1 ?   (D)
72. Which town is at point number 2 ?   (E)
73. Which town is at point number 3 ?   (A)
74. Which town is at point number 4 ?   (F)
75. Which town is at point number 5 ?   (B)
76. Which town is at point number 6 ?   (C)

A certain month has 5 Wednesdays and the 6th. of the month is a Sunday.

77. What date is the third Thursday of the month ? (_____)
78. How many Saturdays are there in the month ? (_____)
79. What day is the 26th. of the month ? (_____)
80. How many Tuesdays are there in the month ? (_____)

**5 children Tom, Roger, Liz, Belle and Sam stand in a circle holding hands. Only one child faces outwards.
Roger holds Tom's right hand in his left and Sam's right hand in his right hand. Liz is not beside Tom and Belle is not beside Sam.**

81. Which child is between Sam and Belle ? (_____)
82. Which two children are holding each other's left hand ? (_____) & (_____)
83. Who is holding Liz's right hand ? (_____)
84. Which girl is closest to Sam ? (_____)
85. Sam leaves the circle and the others close together. Which hand, left or right, and whose hand is Roger now holding with his right hand ? (_____)

	Mon 11th	Tues 12th	Wed 13th	Thurs 14th	Fri 15th	Sat 16th
CUBS	57	19	76	67	73	49
BROWNIES	29	35	56	66	37	58
SCOUTS	27	26	76	47	36	114

This table shows the numbers of Cubs, Brownies and Scouts who went to see Peter Pan in December 1990. The dates of the days are given.

86. On which day and date were there twice as many Scouts at Peter Pan as there were Cubs on Mon 11th. ? (_____)
87. On which day and date did most Brownies attend Peter Pan ? (_____)
88. On which day and date did the number of Brownies and Scouts added together equal the number of Cubs attending Peter Pan ? (_____)
89. On which day and date were there 27 less Cubs at Peter Pan than attended on Wed 13th ? (_____)
90. How many Brownies attended Peter Pan throughout the whole week ? (_____)

TEST 16 PAGE 6.

There are 5 farmers A, B, C, D and E who each have a different number of bulls. No farmer has more than 18 or less than 11 bulls.

C has 3 bulls less than A.
If you added A's bulls to C's bulls you would have 3 times as many bulls as E has.
B does not have more bulls than D.
A is the only person who has an even number of bulls.

91. How many bulls does A have?   (18)

92. How many bulls does B have?   (13)

93. How many bulls does C have?   (15)

94. How many bulls does D have?   (17)

95. How many bulls does E have?   (11)

When it is 1600 hours in London, Moscow is 5 hours ahead of London. New York is 10 hours behind Moscow. A plane leaving Moscow takes 14 hours to fly to and refuel on its way to New York. A plane leaving Moscow takes 4 hours to fly to London. All planes spend 2 hours in London to refuel.

96. If a plane leaves Moscow at 1500 hours (local time) what time will it arrive in New York? (local time)   (1900)

97. What time (local time) will the same plane leave London for New York?   (1600)

98. Another plane arrives in New York from Moscow at 0300 hours (local time) on a Monday. What time (local time) and what day did it leave Moscow?   (2300 Sunday)

99. What time and day did the same plane leave London? (local time)   (0000 Monday)

100. If the time in New York is 1200 hours (local time) What is the time in London?   (1700)

TEST 17

SCORE _____

1. Which letter occurs once in MARBLE but twice in CONCRETE ? (_____)

2. Which letter occurs twice in RECTANGLE but only once in TRIANGLE ? (_____)

3. Which letter occurs three times in PARALLELOGRAM and three times in QUADRILATERAL ? (_____)

4. Half of a number added to 8 is 7 less than 28. What is the number ? (_____)

5. A pencil costs twice as much as a rubber. 4 pencils and a rubber cost 90 pence. How much is a rubber ? (_____)

In the questions below TWO words must change places so that the sentence makes sense. Underline the TWO words that must change places.
Look at this example: The <u>wood</u> was made of <u>table</u>.

6. Start at the end and finish at the beginning.

7. Learning is the key to reading.

8. Was money the locked in the drawer ?

9. The racing car burst on flames into impact.

10. Only computers make mistakes, not humans.

The table below gives some information about the division of numbers in the top row by those in the left hand column.
Complete the table correctly using only the numbers given.

7.8, 25.0, 6.15, 3.0, 12.3.

	÷	75.0	15.6	
11.				
12, 13.			5.2	4.1
14, 15.	2.0	37.5		

In the questions below one word can be put in front of the other words to form four new words. Write the correct word in the brackets.
Look at this example:

	FLY	PROOF	WORKS	MAN	(FIRE)
16.	LOW	LONG	SIDE	HIND	(_____)
17.	DOG	DOZE	FROG	FIGHT	(_____)
18.	FIRE	WARDS	WASH	WATER	(_____)
19.	LONG	ACHE	LIGHT	LINE	(_____)
20.	WRIGHT	THING	ABLE	HOUSE	(_____)

In each line below write in the brackets one letter which completes the word in front of and the word after the brackets.
Look at this example: ROA (D) OOR

21.   SHOWE   (_____)   EED

22.   HAL   (_____)   LAP

23.   PART   (_____)   ARD

24.   DUM   (_____)   ALM

25.   GAUG   (_____)   RUPT

In each line below underline TWO words, ONE from each side, which together make ONE correctly spelt word. The word on the left always comes first. Look at this example:

BLACK ALL TOP   AND **BIRD** BOY

26. PULL   OUT   PUT   FLAP   LET   IN

27. MAN   LAST NOW   AND   HELP AGE

28. CAN   CAT   CAR   HIS   CASE HIM

29. OUT   COT   SHE   TON   BED   IN

30. AT   ON   AS   VEST   TONE TACK

In each question below one letter can be removed from the word in the first column and put into the word in the second column to give two new words. The order of the letters is not changed.
Look at this example:
THINS   TOUT   (THIN)   (STOUT)

31. LATHER   ATE   (_____)   (_____)

32. HARPY   EAST   (_____)   (_____)

33. MINCE   KIT   (_____)   (_____)

34. FRILL   CHAT   (_____)   (_____)

35. POINT   HARD   (_____)   (_____)

5 children A, B, C, D and E are all different ages.
D is older than one other child.
C is younger than one other child.
E is not the oldest or the youngest.
A is older than at least one other child.
List the children in order of age starting with the youngest.

36. (_____) youngest.

37. (_____)

38. (_____)

39. (_____)

40. (_____) oldest.

6 children A, B, C, D, E and F sit equally spaced around a circular table. The table has place settings marked U,V,W,X,Y and Z. The settings are marked clockwise from 12 o'clock starting with U at 12 o'clock.
D sits at the place marked Y and directly opposite the person on A's left. A sits opposite the person on E's left but not beside B. F is not opposite E.

41. Who sits at the place marked U ?   (___A___)

42. Who sits at the place marked V ?   (___F___)

43. Who sits at the place marked W ?   (___E___)

44. Who sits at the place marked X ?   (___B___)

45. Who sits at the place marked Z ?   (___C___)

In the paragraph below five words are missing. Choose the most appropriate words from the lists below. One word from list A fills the space at A, one word from list B fills the space at B and so on.

Underline the word you choose.

The (A) entered his warm (B) where he had been carefully tending his young flowers. He was (C) to find that his assistant had failed to give the flowers (D) and that the loose soil was very (E).

A.	B.	C.	D.	E.
PLUMBER	HALL	HAPPY	WATER	WET
FARMER	SITTING ROOM	ANNOYED	FOOD	HARD
<u>FLORIST</u>	HUT	LAUGHING	GRASS	COLD
DOCTOR	<u>GREEN HOUSE</u>	SMILING	SOIL	DAMP
JOINER	CAR	CHEERFUL	SNOW	<u>DRY</u>
46.	47.	48. <u>ANNOYED</u>	49. <u>WATER</u>	50.

In each question 51-56 the numbers in the second column are formed from the numbers in the first column by using a certain rule. Put the correct answer opposite the arrow. A different rule is used in each question.

51. 3.5----->0
     6.4----->5.8
     7.6----->8.2
     9.4-----> **11.8**

52. 36----->11
     100----->15
     144----->17
     9-----> **8**

53. 3----->4
     6----->8
     9----->12
     15-----> **20**

54. 5----->20
     7----->24
     8----->26
     9-----> **28**

55. 3----->8.5
     4----->9
     5----->9.5
     10-----> **12**

56. 15----->1
     21----->3
     12----->0
     27-----> **5**

Write in the brackets a word that rhymes with the second word and has a similar meaning to the first word.

Look at this example: SICK MILL (__ILL___)

57. INTERVAL   HULL   (_____)
58. UNIT   BUN   (_____)
59. STOP   FAULT (_____)
60. BLAME   FUSE   (_____)
61. CARTON   FOX   (_____)
62. RUBBISH   TASTE (_____)

Complete the sequence by inserting the correct number in the brackets.

63. 16, 24, 20, 28, 24   (_____)
64. 4.9, 6.1, 7.5, 9.1   (_____)
65. 80, 85, 95, 110, 130   (_____)
66. 625, 636, 647, 658   (_____)
67. 740, 739, 735, 726   (_____)
68. 39, 39, 34, 43, 29, 47   (_____)

69. A right-angled triangle has sides of 4cms and 8cms which touch to form a right-angle. What is half of its area? (_____)

70. A circle can be drawn inside a square so that the circle just touches all four sides of the square. If the square has an area of 25 sq. cms. what is the radius of the circle? (_____)

These questions are about the following shapes.

**REGULAR PENTAGON, SQUARE,
RIGHT-ANGLED TRIANGLE, RECTANGLE.**

Use this information only and answer these questions.

71. Which shape or shapes do not have all internal angles the same? (_____)

72. Which shape has most sides? (_____)

73. Which shape or shapes could not be cut into 2 right-angled triangles using only one cut? (_____)

74. Which shape or shapes could you not be sure would have at least one line of symmetry? (_____)

Questions 75 - 78 are about the lines drawn inside the squares.

A   B   C   D   E

75. Name one square which has lines crossing at 45 degrees. (_____)

76,77. Name two squares with parallel lines. (_____) & (_____)

78. Name one square in which lines cross at right-angles. (_____)

**Three farmers Mark, Sam and Paul each have a cow, a goat and a horse. There is one of each animal in three different colours. The colours are white, brown and black.
No farmer has two animals of the same colour.**

**Sam's cow is the same colour as Mark's goat.
Paul's cow is the same colour as Sam's goat.
Sam's horse is brown. Mark's horse is black.**

79. Who has a white horse ? (_____)

80. Who has a white goat ? (_____)

81. Who has a white cow ? (_____)

82. What colour is Sam's goat ? (_____)

83. What colour is Mark's cow ? (_____)

84. What colour is Paul's goat ? (_____)

**Six tins of coloured paint are on a shelf.
The green and orange are at the ends. Only pink, which is not beside orange, comes between the black and an end colour. Blue is not beside black but is further to the left. The other colour is red. List the colours, starting at the left.**

85. (_____) left

86. (_____)

87. (_____)

88. (_____)

89. (_____)

90. (_____) right

TEST 17 PAGE 5.

Five children A, B, C, D and E are playing with cards numbered 0-9. The children each turn over five cards and then total their scores. The child nearest to zero wins the game.

The rules are as follows.

If a child turns over 0 he subtracts 9 from his total. If two children turn over the same card the number turned over is doubled and added on. If three children turn over the same card the number shown is not counted in the total. All other numbers are added.

The children turn over these cards.

A.	8	9	6	1	2
B.	3	8	7	6	4
C.	6	0	5	9	3
D.	0	9	1	2	3
E.	1	2	0	8	5

91. Which child won the game ? (_____)

92. Which child was last ? (_____)

93. What was C's score ? (_____)

94. What was E's score ? (_____)

95. What was D's score ? (_____)

Five people Joe, Dot, Ann, Sam and June had birthdays on the 2nd January 1990.
Joe is 5 years older than Sam who is half as old as Dot. Ann is twice as old as Dot but only 1 year older than June. In 7 years time June will be 34 years old.

96. What age was Sam 5 years ago ? (_____)

97. How many years will it be before Sam is as old as Ann is now ? (_____)

98. What age is Dot now ? (_____)

99. What age was June 9 years ago ? (_____)

100. What total would I get if I added all their ages together ? (_____)

TEST 17 PAGE 6.

TEST 18

SCORE _____

1. Which letter occurs as often in BEGINNING as it does in GRABBING ? (_____)

2. Which letter appears once in UNDERSTANDING, twice in PERMISSION but not at all in THOUSANDS ? (_____)

3. Which letter occurs half as many times in REASONED as it does in GOVERNMENT ? (_____)

4. One third of a certain number is the same as one quarter of 60. What is the number ? (_____)

If Tim had 6p more he would have half as much as Jill. Jill has 3 times as much as Fred who is 12p short of 30p. How much does each one have ?

5. Tim.   (_____)

6. Jill.   (_____)

7. Fred.   (_____)

In the sentences below 2 words must change places to make the sentences sensible. Underline the TWO words. An example is shown.

The <u>woo</u>d is made of <u>table</u>.

8. This time Elizabeth week next will be twelve.

9. The smoking of was in need chimney cleaning.

10. Broke the storm the clouds after up.

11. Cars park unable to were in the busy street.

12. Two boys number their coats on peg hung ten.

13. Slowly sailed ship the silently into port.

The table below gives some information about the addition of numbers in the left hand column to numbers in the top row. Complete the table.

14.
15, 16, 17.
18, 19.

+		5.5	7.6
11.9			
8.7	17.4		

TEST 18 PAGE 1.

In each question write in the brackets one letter which will complete both the word in front of the brackets and the word after the brackets.

Here is an example.   ROA (D) OOR.

20. HUL ( ) ERB   21. DIA ( ) OAN

22. FAD ( ) STATE   23. LAS ( ) OME

24. TO ( ) RACE   25. WAR ( ) USK

In each line below a word from the left-hand group joins one from the right-hand group to make a new word. The left-hand word comes first. Underline the chosen words. An example has been done to help you.

CORN   FARM   TIME   **OVER   FIELD   YARD**

26.   PANE   SNAP   SET   LAST   MAD   PING
27.   BAR   ON   FARE   SON   GAIN WORD
28.   HEAD   OVER   FOR   TURN   ROW   DRAWER
29.   PALM   FOE   OUT   THUS   LET   TIN
30.   MAIN   FALL   HAS   BODY   IT   LAND
31.   EVER   INN   LET   SIDE   TING YEAR

In the following questions a letter can be taken from the first word and put into the second word to form TWO new words. Write both NEW words.

Example. THEN   TANK   (TEN) (THANK)

The H moves from THEN to TANK and makes the new words TEN and THANK.

32.   DICE   PATH   (_____) (_____)
33.   STREAM CAT   (_____) (_____)
34.   FLAIR   HAVE   (_____) (_____)
35.   PAINT   BAT   (_____) (_____)
36.   GANG   LACE   (_____) (_____)
37.   TAMPER SANK   (_____) (_____)

TEST 18 PAGE 2.

F, G, H, I, J and K are six boats sailing due SOUTH in a race.
H is due east of G.   J is due south of F.
I is due west of J.   G is due south of J and due north of K.

38. Which boat is leading in the race? (K)

39. Which boat is last in the race? (F)

40. How many boats are further to the south than J? (3)

41. Which boat is sailing furthest east? (H)

42. Which boat is sailing furthest west? (I)

Groups of words are printed below. Each group is made up of words which are similar in some way.

A	B	C	D	E	F
padre	spear	hull	post	roast	rope
minister	lance	rudder	stop	boil	string
priest	javelin	bridge	tops	fry	cord

Decide into which of the above groups the following words would fit. Write the group letter in the brackets.

43. pots (D)   44. twine (F)

45. stew (E)   46. pastor (A)

47. pike (B)   48. keel (C)

In a code words are written as shown below.

ORIENTAL becomes ABCDEFGH   **BUGGY becomes IJKKL**

Write the following words in code.

49. IGNORANT (CKEABGEF)   50. TANGERINE (FGEKDBCED)

Decode the following words.

51. DEGIHD (ENABLE)   52. KGCDFL (GAIETY)

53. GFFABEDL (ATTORNEY)   54. HGEKJGKD (LANGUAGE)

The information below is about 4 boys W, X, Y, and Z and the drinks that they like.

W and X are the only two who like both milk and lemonade.
X and Z are the only two who like both lemonade and tea.
Y and W are the only two who like both fruit juice and coffee.

55. Which drink does W not like ?   (_____)

56. Who likes coffee but not lemonade ?   (_____)

57. Who likes lemonade, tea and milk ?   (_____)

58. Who likes lemonade but not tea ?   (_____)

59. Who likes coffee and fruit juice but not milk ? (_____)

60. Which drink is the most popular?   (_____)

In a month there were 4 Wednesdays. The 19th of the month was a Saturday.

61. What day was the 1st of the month ?   (_____)

62. What date was the third Sunday ?   (_____)

63. Which month could it be ? (May, February or April)   (_____)

64. What date was the last Friday of the previous month ?   (_____)

65. What day was the 20th of the previous month ?   (_____)

Complete the following sequences. The alphabet is printed to help you.

A B C D E F G H I J K L M N O P Q R S T U V W X Y Z

66.   A   Y   B   W   C   (_____)

67.   B   E   G   J   L   (_____)

68.   FL   MG   HN   OI   (_____)

69.   CCX VDD EET RFF   (_____)

70.   BDC EGF HJI KML   (_____)

71.   ZRC ESY XTG IUW   (_____)

TEST 18 PAGE 4.

In each of the following questions 3 words are in alphabetical order.
The second word has not been written but its meaning is given.
Decide what the second word should be each time and write it in the
brackets. Each dash in the brackets represents a letter.
An example is shown to help you.

CROSS

(C R O W D) a large group of people.

CRUEL

72. MIRROR

   (_ _ _ _ _) person who hoards money.

   MITTEN

73. HASTY

   (_ _ _ _ _ _) short, light axe.

   HAUNT

74. ORANGE

   (_ _ _ _ _) path of a planet around the sun.

   OSTRICH

75. STRONG

   (_ _ _ _ _ _) artist's work-room.

   STUTTER

76. LANTERN

   (_ _ _ _ _ _) storage room for food.

   LATCH

77. COMFORT

   (_ _ _ _ _) humorous, funny.

   CONCEAL

TEST 18 PAGE 5.

Six different types of fruit were displayed side by side on a shelf in the window of a fruit shop.

The bananas were beside the apples and the grapes.
Neither the pears nor the grapes were at the end of the shelf.
The apples were not beside the oranges or the pears.
The oranges were furthest from the left.
The melons and one other fruit were in the middle of the shelf.

List the fruit in order from left to right.

(__apples__) (__bananas__) (__grapes__) (__melons__) (__pears__) (__oranges__)
  left   right

78.   79.   80.   81.   82.   83.

Together Pete, Anne, Rose and Fred have £64.
Rose has £3 less than Pete who has £5 more than Fred.
Fred has £5 less than Anne.

84. How much has Pete? (£18)

85. How much has Anne? (£18)

86. How much has Rose? (£15)

87. How much has Fred? (£13)

Using the numbers 2, 3, 4 and 6 ONCE ONLY in each question, fill in the spaces in a way that will make the statements correct.
An example is shown to help you.

     _2_ + _3_ + _4_ + _6_ = 15.

88. (_2_ + _3_) − (_6_ − _4_) = 3.

89. (_3_ + _4_ + _6_) × _2_ = 26.

90. (_2_ + _6_) × (_4_ − _3_) = 8.

91. (_3_ × _4_) − (_6_ − _2_) = 8.

92. (_3_ − _2_) + (_4_ × _6_) = 25.

93. Arthur's house. (6)   94. Barry's house. (7)

95. Christine's house. (2)   96. David's house. (3)

97. Edith's house. (4)   98. Fred's house. (1)

99. George's house. (8)   100. Harry's house. (5)

TEST 19

SCORE _____

1. Which letter appears the same number of times in the words REMEMBER
   and ENFORCEMENT ? (____)

2. Which letter is in the word PRESIDENT but not in the word DEPRESSION? (____)

3. Which letter occurs twice as often in PARTICULAR as it does in SECRETARY? (____)

4. Six times a number is four more than twice 19. What is the number ? (____)

**In three years Alan will be twice as old as Bob was last year.
Colin, who will be 5 next year, is 2 years younger than Bob.
How old is each boy ?**

5. Alan   (____)

6. Bob   (____)

7. Colin   (____)

In the sentences below 2 words must change places to make the sentences sensible. Underline the TWO words. An example is shown.

The <u>wood</u> is made of <u>table</u>.

8. Tom's watch and one was a half minutes fast.

9. The aeroplane flew just above an ground.

10. The bay was in rough for fishing too.

11. I to not reach could the top shelf.

12. Always before food well chew swallowing it.

13. Peter hugged long his lost brother.

The table below gives some information about the addition of numbers in the left hand column to numbers in the top row. Complete the table.

14, 15.
16, 17.
18, 19.

+	8.7		
12.6		26.4	
	18.1		20

TEST 19 PAGE 1.

In each question write in the brackets one letter which will complete both the word in front of the brackets and the word after the brackets.

Here is an example.   ROA (D) OOR.

20.   CAME ( ) ENS   21.   TAR ( ) ASK

22.   GE   ( ) AID   23.   SCA ( ) ACK

24.   FAN ( ) ABLE   25.   TAL ( ) ALM

In each line below a word from the left-hand group joins one from the right-hand group to make a new word. The left-hand word comes first. Underline the chosen words. An example has been done to help you.

    CORN   **FARM**   TIME   OVER   FIELD   **YARD**

26.   AIM   OVER   OUT   RING   PUT   TEAR
27.   BAND   OR   GET   IT   GILL   BUT
28.   FOR   SUM   TO   WORK   LET   WING
29.   OVER   DEAD   COME   SON   LOCK   LEE
30.   BE   SET   RAN   LESS   PANT   SACK
31.   PORT   CORD   NO   ABLE   TAIL   HEAD

In the following questions a letter can be taken from the first word and put into the second word to form TWO new words. Write both NEW words.

Example.   THEN   TANK   (TEN) (THANK)

The H moves from THEN to TANK and makes the new words TEN and THANK.

32.   NIECE   PACE   (_____) (_____)
33.   BARON   NOSE   (_____) (_____)
34.   YEAR   EARL   (_____) (_____)
35.   MANAGER   HAD   (_____) (_____)
36.   GAUNT   BARE   (_____) (_____)
37.   PART   GEM   (_____) (_____)

TEST 19 PAGE 2.

38. First in the left-hand lane. (red)

39. Second in the left-hand lane. (red)

40. First in the right-hand lane. (yellow)

41. Second in the right-hand lane. (green)

42. Third in the right-hand lane. (orange)

43. Fourth in the right-hand lane. (black)

44. A: **off**

45. B: **match**

46. C: **dark**

47. D: **faint**

48. E: **lit**

49. F: **house**

The table below shows the number of people in various age groups in four villages called Sulby, Picton, Marlow and Widford.

Age group A - Up to 18 years of age.
Age group B - From 19 to 60 years of age.
Age group C - Over 60 years of age.

Age Group	SULBY	PICTON	MARLOW	WIDFORD
A	550	400	120	420
B	700	530	400	530
C	270	310	320	310

50. Which age group A, B or C has the greatest number of people ?   (_____)

51. Which age group A, B or C has the smallest number of people ?   (_____)

52. Which village has more than half as many people in group A as in groups B and C together ?   (_____)

53. Which village has one third of its population in group A ?   (_____)

54. Which village has one quarter of its population in group C ?   (_____)

In the questions below give the next number in each series.

55.   2   5   11   23   (_____)

56.   8.8   7.2   5.6   4   (_____)

57.   80   63   48   35   (_____)

58.   (4, 9)   (11, 23)   (18, 37)   (____,____)

59.   (27, 3)   (21, 7)   (15, 11)   (____,____)

TEST 19 PAGE 4.

Six children, A, B, C, D, E and F stand equally spaced in a circle.
They face into the centre of the circle.
Two other children G and H stand in the centre of the circle with their backs to one another.
H is facing directly at C. G is facing directly at F who is closer to D than he is to E.   A is between C and D and E is on the left of B.
Everyone makes a half turn and faces the opposite way.

60. Who is standing directly behind G ?   (F)

61. Who is standing directly behind H ?   (C)

62. Who is to the left of F ?   (D)

63. Who is to the right of E ?   (C)

64. Who is furthest from D ?   (E)

65. Who is furthest from B ?   (A)

In each of the following questions find a word which has a similar meaning to the left-hand word and rhymes with the right-hand word.

Example   TREMBLE   RIVER   (SHIVER)

SHIVER rhymes with RIVER and means TREMBLE.

66. MAIDEN   WHIRL   (GIRL)
67. RATION   FAIR   (SHARE)
68. FAITHFUL   CLUE   (TRUE)
69. CABLE   TYRE   (WIRE)
70. SHIP   NOTE   (BOAT)
71. CONSTRUCT   ACHE   (MAKE)

In the following questions the numbers in the second column are formed from the numbers in the first column by using the same rule. Put the correct answer in the brackets for each question.

72. 3 ----> 14   73. 12 ----> 1   74. 2 ----> 7
     7 ----> 22   15 ----> 2   3 ----> 26
    10 ----> 28   24 ----> 5   4 ----> 63

    20 ----> (48)   30 ----> (7)   5 ----> (124)

75. 4 ----> 6   76. 4 ----> 3   77. 2 ----> 5
     7 ----> 12   14 ----> 8   4 ----> 17
    11 ----> 20   20 ----> 11   7 ----> 50

    24 ----> (46)   30 ----> (16)   9 ----> (82)

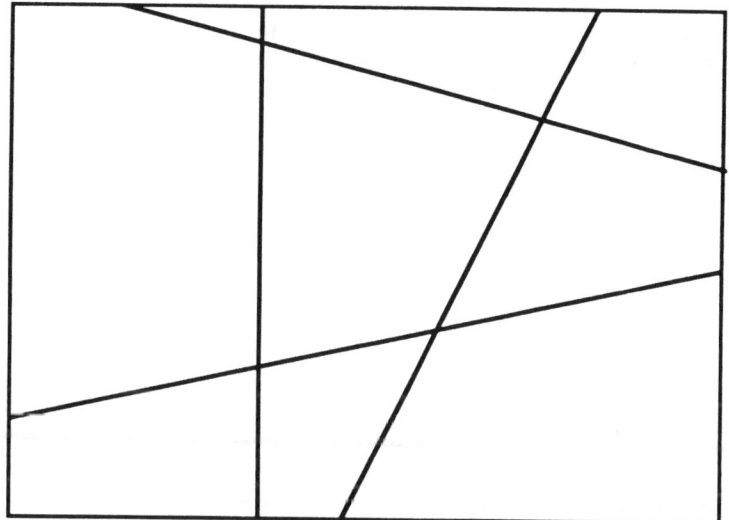

State whether the following statements about the diagram above are true or false. Write T for true or F for false in the brackets.

78. There are more than 6 right angles. (_____)

79. There are more than 6 triangles. (_____)

80. There are 3 lines parallel to one another. (_____)

81. There are 3 horizontal lines ? (_____)

82. One of the lines divides the diagram into two equal pieces. (_____)

Six people live in a row of 6 houses numbered 1, 2, 3, 4, 5 and 6.
The people are called Adams, Black, Carr, Davis, Evans and Fee.
There are 2 people between Carr and Davis.
Fee lives at one end of the row with 3 people between him and Adams.
Black lives further from Fee than from Adams.
Davis and Black live beside one another.
Fee lives closer to number 3 than to number 4.
Give the number of each person's house.

83. Which house does Adams live in ? (_____)

84. Which house does Black live in ? (_____)

85. Which house does Carr live in ? (_____)

86. Which house does Davis live in ? (_____)

87. Which house does Evans live in ? (_____)

88. Which house does Fee live in ? (_____)

Four girls E, F, G and H played with a set of 20 cards.
The cards had single numbers printed on them.
There were 5 cards for each of the numbers 1, 2, 3 and 4. The cards were mixed up and shared out equally.
Each girl added together the numbers on her cards and the winner was the one with the highest total.
The first 3 cards for each girl are shown below.

Girl E.   4, 1, 2
Girl F.   2, 2, 4
Girl G.   3, 1, 3
Girl H.   3, 2, 4

One child had only odd numbers and another had only even numbers.
F and H tied for first place with the same score.
G's last two cards were the same and she finished last.

89. What did H score ?   (14)

90. What did E score ?   (13)

91. What did G score ?   (9)

If the cards marked 1 had been marked 5 instead, who would have been -

92. First ?   (G)

93. Second ?   (H)

94. Third ?   (E)

95. Last ?   (F)

Three girls Nora, Pat and Lynn each have a lunch box, a pencil case and a purse. The objects are coloured blue, yellow or red.
Each lunch box is a different colour, as are the pencil cases and purses.
Each girl's three objects are of a different colour.

Pat's purse and Nora's lunch box are the same colour.
Lynn's purse, Pat's lunch box and Nora's pencil case are all the same colour. Lynn's lunch box is blue and her pencil case is not red.

96. What colour is Lynn's pencil case ?   (yellow)

97. What colour is Pat's lunch box ?   (red)

98. What colour is Nora's purse ?   (blue)

99. Which girl has the red pencil case ?   (Nora)

100. Which girl has the yellow purse ?   (Pat)

TEST 20

SCORE _____

1. Which letter occurs as often in EPIDEMIC as it does in EPICURE, and also occurs twice in DISCONNECT? (_____)

2. Which letter, occuring once in GASTRONOMY, occurs twice in GASTRONOMIST and twice in GAZETTE? (_____)

3. Which letter in GEANTICLINE occurs more than once and is closest to the end of the alphabet? (_____)

4. When 6 is subtracted from a number it gives an answer which is 5 more than 29. What is the number? (_____)

A cake costs 18p more than a packet of biscuits. Together they cost 96p.

5. How much is a cake? (_____)

6. How much is a packet of biscuits? (_____)

**In the questions below TWO words must change places so that the sentence makes sense. Underline the TWO words that must change places.
Look at this example: The <u>wood</u> was made of <u>table</u>.**

7. The neighbours that complained the music was too loud.

8. The was garage left open and unattended?

9. The sweet cake was laden with a beautiful trolley.

10. Three ambulances arrived within the minutes of the accident.

11. I could not the find word in my dictionary.

12. Air up are going fares next month.

The table below gives some information about the subtraction of numbers in the left hand column from those in the top row. Complete the table correctly.

13.	—		3.9
14.		4.7	2.3
15.	2.9		1.0
16, 17.		2.4	

In each line below write in the brackets one letter which completes the word in front of and the word after the brackets. Look at this example:
    ROA (D) OOR

18.   RHYTH (____) URMUR

19.   SLAN (____) HEFT

20.   SHEE (____) INTH

21.   STA   (____) OLK

22.   POR   (____) LOPE

23.   CUR   (____) AID

TEST 20 PAGE 1.

In each line below underline TWO words, ONE from each side, which together make ONE correctly spelt word. The word on the left always comes first. Look at this example:

BL<u>ACK</u> ALL TOP   AND **<u>BIR</u>D** BOY

24.   AS   AFTER   AGO   GO   TASTE   MOON
25.   SEE   SAW   SAT   TED   DING   PAY
26.   NO   SERF   OF   VICE   ALL   PUT
27.   ARE   FEAT   CUT   HIM   BIT   HER
28.   HUM   OR   RIB   BUD   AN   GAIN
29.   COT   FLAT   PORT   TEN   END   TEND

In each question below, two consecutive letters can be removed from the word in the first column and put into the word in the second column to give two new words. The order of the letters is not changed and the two consecutive letters remain together.
Look at this example: GIR<u>DLE</u>   ASH   (GIRD)   (<u>L</u>ASH)

30.   HANDLE   BED   (_____)   (_____)
31.   CARPET   HELD   (_____)   (_____)
32.   BEDROOM   IT   (_____)   (_____)
33.   PILLOW   BELL   (_____)   (_____)
34.   FLOWER   BET   (_____)   (_____)

In questions 35-40 the three words A, B and C are in alphabetical order. The word at B is missing and you are given a dictionary definition instead. Write the correct word in the space.
Look at this example: A) FLAP
                         B) (FLARE) Distress signal from a boat.
                         C) FLASH

35. (A) NETTLE
    (B) (_ _ _ _ _ _) Not favouring either side.
    (C) NEVER

36. (A) BEVERAGE
    (B) (_ _ _ _ _) Be on one's guard.
    (C) BEWITCH

37. (A) SALAMANDER
    (B) (_ _ _ _ _) Fixed payment made to a person.
    (C) SALIVA

38. (A) THE
    (B) (_ _ _ _ _ _) A structure for showing drama.
    (C) THEIR

39. (A) PROSTRATE
    (B) (_ _ _ _ _ _) To guard from danger.
    (C) PROTEST

40. (A) STRIKE
    (B) (_ _ _ _ _) Fine cord.
    (C) STRIPE

TEST 20 PAGE 2.

The words below, and those in the lists, are alike in some way. Write the letter of the list that each word belongs to in the brackets. Each letter may be used only once.

A	**B**	**C**	**D**	**E**
FEZ	CROWD	QUAY	CUB	BAT
CROWN	RABBLE	DOCK	FOAL	FOX
BERET	GANG	HARBOUR	DUCKLING	HORSE

41. WHARF   (C)

42. CYGNET   (D)

43. TURBAN   (A)

44. WHALE   (E)

45. MOB   (B)

Six soldiers A, B, C, D, E and F were marching in line one behind the other. There were two soldiers in front of B and none behind A. D was 3 places behind C who was 4 places in front of A. F was nearer the front of the line than E was. The soldiers stopped, made a half turn, and marched off in the opposite direction.
List the soldiers in order from first to last.

46. (A) First.

47. (D)

48. (E)

49. (B)

50. (C)

51. (F) Last.

Using the numbers 7, 8, 5, and 4 once only in each question fill in the spaces in any way which makes the statements correct.

52.   (7 X 5) - (8 X 4) = 3

53.   (8 - 5) - (7 - 4) = 0

54.   (8 + 5 - 7) X 4   = 24

TEST 20 PAGE 3.

A, B, C and D are four shops.
Only A and D are open late in the evenings and are closed on Sundays.
Only B and C have self-service and have a sale on at present.
Only D and B are closed on Sundays and have self-service.

55. Which shop is closed on Sunday and is not self-service ? (_____)

56. Which self-service shop has a sale but closes on Sunday ? (_____)

57. Which shop closes early and on Sunday ? (_____)

58. Which shop opens on Sunday and has a sale ? (_____)

59. Could you buy something in shop D late on a Sunday ? (_____)

60. Is there a self-service shop open late ? (_____)

	BREAM	ROACH	PIKE
ENGLAND	65	44	132
IRELAND	127.5	32.5	40
FRANCE	70	122.6	63.75

The above table shows the weight (in kgs.) of three different types of fish caught by three fishing teams in a fishing contest.

61. Which team caught half the weight in pike as Ireland caught in bream ? (_____)

62. Which team caught 3 times as much weight in pike as England caught in roach ? (_____)

63. Which team caught 1/5th of its total weight of fish in pike ? (_____)

64. Which team's catch of bream was twice as heavy as Ireland's catch of roach ? (_____)

65. Which team caught 3/4's as much again in bream as Ireland caught in pike ? (_____)

Complete these sequences by inserting the correct letter(s) or number(s) in the brackets. The alphabet is printed to help you.

A B C D E F G H I J K L M N O P Q R S T U V W X Y Z

66. 121, 81, 49, 25   (_____)

67. 104, 156, 208, 260   (_____)

68. 4.70, 7.05, 9.40, 11.75   (_____)

69. B, D, G, I   (_____)

70. DBC, GEF, JHI, MKL   (_____)

71. XBD, FCV, TDH, JER   (_____)

A farmer has 104 animals. He has 18 more pigs than sheep and 5 fewer sheep than cows.

72. How many cows has he ?   (_____)

73. How many pigs has he ?   (_____)

74. How many sheep has he ?   (_____)

75. If he exchanged 1/3rd of his pigs for 8 sheep and 2 cows how many animals would he have ?   (_____)

Six towns A, B, C, D, E and F are at the points marked 1-6 but not in that order. The arrow points to North.

NORTH <==========================

```
              4       5
              X       X

       1      2
       X      X

              3       6
              X       X
```

Town C is one of the most Southerly towns. Town E is due West of town D which is due South of town B, which in turn has no towns further North. Town F is not East of town D or South of town A.

76. Which town is at point number 1 ?   (_____)

77. Which town is at point number 2 ?   (_____)

78. Which town is at point number 3 ?   (_____)

79. Which town is at point number 4 ?   (_____)

80. Which town is at point number 5 ?   (_____)

81. Which town is at point number 6 ?   (_____)

In a certain code

DISCOUNT is written as HMWGSYRX
JANUARY is written as NERYEVC
MATCHES is written as QEXGLIW

The alphabet is printed to help you.

A B C D E F G H I J K L M N O P Q R S T U V W X Y Z

What are these words in code?

82. POLISH (_____)

83. SECRET (_____)

84. TALKING (_____)

Decode these words.

85. IRKMRI (_____)

86. EYXLSV (_____)

A girl was given a packet of sweets which were various colours.
The colours were black, white, yellow, red, green, blue, purple and orange.
There was a different number of each colour and no more than 8 of any one colour.
There were twice as many white sweets as purple sweets and half as many red sweets as blue sweets. There were more orange sweets than black sweets and 3 more green sweets than purple sweets.
The girl decided to eat all the black and green sweets and that would have left 27. However she changed her mind and ate all the black and yellow ones instead and had 23 left.

How many sweets of each colour did she start with?

87. BLACK (_____)

88. WHITE (_____)

89. YELLOW (_____)

90. RED (_____)

91. GREEN (_____)

92. BLUE (_____)

93. PURPLE (_____)

94. ORANGE (_____)

TEST 20 PAGE 6.

95. HORSE   (Pat)
96. LION   (John)
97. TIGER   (Sarah)
98. MONKEY   (Tim)
99. OSTRICH   (David)
100. ELEPHANT (Liz)

Answers to Test 16

1. L
2. R
3. E
4. 36
5. 160
6. THEIR
7. IN
8. FINS
9. SICK
10. CATTLE
11. 7.3
12. 4.9
13. 7.1
14. 1.6
15. 5.7
16. SHUT
17. TREAD
18. HERD
19. EAR
20. SORT
21. S
22. T
23. N
24. E
25. T
26. IN
27. NO
28. BUTTER
29. SAT
30. PASS
31. JET
32. HOUND
33. FIND
34. ZCDMPC
35. BYLECP
36. LYNIGL
37. GROUP
38. EMERGE
39. CALCULATE
40. 6
41. 0
42. 30
43. 3
44. 4
45. Y
46. W
47. Z
48. X
49. U
50. V

51. ARCHERY
52. ALAN
53. ALAN
54. 2
55. DARREN
56. PREVENT
57. DUTCH
58. SCRATCH
59. MANSE
60. RIOT
61. ALARM
62. D
63. B
64. C
65. A
66. E
67. U
68. S
69. CDD
70. ED
71. D
72. E
73. A
74. F
75. B
76. C
77. 17th
78. 4
79. SATURDAY
80. 5
81. LIZ
82. SAM, LIZ
83. BELLE
84. LIZ
85. LIZ'S LEFT
86. SAT 16th
87. THURS 14th
88. FRI 15th
89. SAT 16th
90. 281
91. 18
92. 13
93. 15
94. 17
95. 11
96. 1900 HOURS
97. 1600 HOURS
98. 2300 HOURS Sunday
99. 0000 HOURS Monday
100. 1700 HOURS

THE
THE
FISH
UNABLE
FORESTS

STOOP
SHOP
SEAT
BOUGHT
PANTS

SCRIBE
ON
CUP
URN
AGE

Answers to Test 17

1. E
2. E
3. A
4. 26
5. ICp
6. END   BEGINNING
7. LEARNING READING
8. MONEY   THE
9. ON   INTO
10. HUMANS   COMPUTERS
11. 12.3
12. 3.0
13. 25.0
14. 7.8
15. 5.15
16. BE
17. BULL
18. BACK
19. HEAD
20. PLAY
21. R or D
22. E
23. Y
24. D or B
25. E
26. OUT   LET
27. MAN   AGE
28. CAR   CASE
29. COT   TON
30. AT   TACK
31. LATER   HATE/LATHE RATE
32. HARP   YEAST
33. MICE   KNIT
34. FILL   CHART
35. PINT   HOARD
36. 3
37. D
38. C
39. C
40. A
41. A
42. E
43. E
44. C
45. E
46. FLORIST
47. GREENHOUSE
48. ANNOYED
49. WATER
50. DRY

51. L
52. 11.8 (2X-7)
53. 8 (SQ ROOT X + 5)
54. 20 (X + 1/3X)
55. 28 2X+10
56. 12 (X+2)+7
57. 5(X+3)-4
58. LULL
59. ONE
60. HALT
61. ACCUSE
62. BOX
63. WASTE
64. 32
65. 10.9
66. 155
67. 669
68. 710
69. 24
70. 8 sq. cms.
71. 2.5 sq cms
72. RIGHT-ANGLED TRI
73. REG. PENTAGON
74. REG. PENT
75. RIGHT-ANGLED TRI
76. A or B
77. B
78. D
79. C
80. PAUL
81. MARK
82. SAM
83. BLACK
84. BROWN
85. BROWN
86. ORANGE
87. BLUE
88. RED
89. BLACK
90. PINK
91. GREEN
92. A
93. B
94. 1
95. -9
96. 2 YEARS
97. 21 YEARS
98. 14 YEARS
99. 18 YEARS
100. 88 YEARS

These are the answers to Book 4 of a set of 4 graded books. A child who has not previously attempted questions of this type may have difficulty with the first few tests. However, research shows that a child's ability to handle and understand these questions generally increases with practice.

Answers to Test 18

1. G
2. I
3. N
4. 45
5. 21
6. 54
7. 18
8. ELIZABETH
9. OF   NEXT
10. BROKE   CHIMNEY
11. PARK   AFTER
12. NUMBER   WERE
13. SAILED   HUNG
14. 8.7   THE
15. 20.6
16. 17.4
17. 19.5
18. 14.2
19. 16.3
20. K
21. E
22. H or S
23. T or G
24. T or D or M
25. SNAP   PING
26. BAR   GAIN
27. OVER   TURN
28. OUT   LET
29. MAIN   LAND
30. LET   TING
31. DIE   PATCH
32. STEAM   CART
33. FAIR   HALVE
34. PANT   BAIT
35. GAG   LANCE
36. TAMER   SPANK
37.
38. F
39. K
40. 3
41. H
42. I
43. D
44. F
45. E
46. A
47. B
48. C
49. CKEABGEF
50. FGEKDBCED

51. ENABLE
52. GAIETY
53. ATTORNEY
54. LANGUAGE
55. TEA
56. Y
57. X
58. W
59. Y
60. LEMONADE
61. TUESDAY
62. 20th FEBRUARY
63. 28th THURSDAY
64.
65.
66. U
67. O
68. JP
69. GGP
70. NPO
71. VVK
72. MISER
73. HATCHET
74. ORBIT
75. STUDIO
76. LARDER
77. COMIC
78. APPLES
79. BANANAS
80. GRAPES
81. MELONS
82. PEARS
83. ORANGES
84. 18
85. 15
86. 13
87. 3, 2, 6, 4
88. 3, 6, 4, 2
89. 6, 2, 4, 3
90. 6, 4, 2, 3
91. 3, 2, 6, 4,
92.
93.
94.
95. 7
96. 3
97. 4
98. 1
99. 8
100. 5

* Other combinations may be correct.

Answers to Test 19

1. E
2. T
3. A
4. 7
5. 6
6. 4
7. AND   WAS
8. THE   AN
9. Y   TOO
10. IN   COULD
11. TO   CHEW
12. BEFORE   HIS
13. LONG
14. 13.8
15. 10.6
16. 21.3
17. 23.2
18. 9.4
19. 23.2
20. L
21. T
22. M
23. R or B
24. G
25. C
26. OUT   PUT
27. BAND   IT
28. TO   WING
29. DEAD   LOCK
30. RAN   SACK
31. PORT   ABLE
32. NICE   PEACE
33. BARN   NOOSE
34. EAR   EARLY
35. MANAGE   HARD
36. AUNT   BARGE
37. PAT   GERM
38. RED
39. RED
40. YELLOW
41. GREEN
42. ORANGE
43. BLACK
44. OFF
45. MATCH
46. DARK
47. FAINT
48. LIT
49. HOUSE
50. B

51. C
52. SULBY
53. WIDFORD
54. PICTON
55. 47
56. 2,4
57. 24
58. 25, 51
59. 9, 15
60. F
61. C
62. D
63. C
64. E
65. A
66. GIRL
67. SHARE
68. TRUE
69. WIRE
70. BOAT
71. MAKE
72. 48 2X+8
73. 7 (X+3)-3
74. 124 X cubed -1
75. 46 2X-2
76. 16 (X+2)+2
77. 82 Xsq+1
78. F
79. F
80. T
81. F
82. T
83. F
84. 4
85. 5
86. 3
87. 2
88. 1
89. 14
90. 13
91. 9
92. G
93. H
94. E
95. D
96. YELLOW
97. RED
98. BLUE
99. NORA
100. PAT

Answers to Test 20

1. C
2. T
3. N
4. 40
5. 57
6. 39
7. THAT   COMPLAINED
8. THE   WAS
9. CAKE   TROLLEY
10. THREE   NO
11. UP   YES
12. THE   FRANCE
13. FIND   ENGLAND
14. FARE   IRELAND
15. 1.6   ENGLAND
16. 3.4   FRANCE
17. 3.9
18. 0.0
19. M
20. T
21. N
22. Y
23. E
24. L
25. SEE   TASTE
26. NO   DING
27. FEAT   VICE
28. HUM   HER
29. FLAT   AN
30. HAND   TEN
31. CART   BLEED
32. BROOM   HELPED
33. PILL   EDIT
34. FLOW   BELLOW
35. NEUTRAL   BERET
36. BEWARE
37. SALARY
38. THEATRE
39. PROTECT
40. STRING
41. C
42. A
43. H
44. E
45. B
46. A
47. D
48. E
49. B
50. C

51. F   7
52. 5   5
53. 4   4
54. 8   8
55. A   5
56. B   7
57. C   4
58. B
59. NO
60. YES
61. FRANCE
62. ENGLAND
63. IRELAND
64. ENGLAND
65. FRANCE
66. 9
67. 312
68. 14.10
69. L
70. PNO
71. PFL
72. 32
73. 45
74. 27
75. 99
76. D
77. B
78. E
79. A
80. C
81. F
82. TSPMWL
83. WIGVIX
84. XEPOMRK
85. ENGINE
86. AUTHOR
87. 2
88. 5
89. 8
90. 3
91. 4
92. 6
93. 1
94. E
95. LIZ
96. SARAH
97. JOHN
98. TIM
99. PAT
100. DAVID

* Other combinations may work

Six animals go round a roundabout in a clockwise direction in this order. Horse, lion, tiger, monkey, ostrich and elephant. The ostrich and the horse also go up and down.
Six children Liz, Pat, Sarah, Tim, John and David pay to have a ride on the roundabout.
Pat's animal goes up and down following David's. Tim rides between the tiger and the ostrich. David is closer to Pat than he is to John. Sarah follows John and her animal only moves in a clockwise direction.

Who rides on which animal ?

95.   HORSE   (Pat)

96.   LION   (John)

97.   TIGER   (Sarah)

98.   MONKEY   (Tim)

99.   OSTRICH   (David)

100.   ELEPHANT   (Liz)

In a certain code

DISCOUNT   is written as HMWGSYRX
JANUARY   is written as NERYEVC
MATCHES   is written as QEXGLIW

The alphabet is printed to help you.

A B C D E F G H I J K L M N O P Q R S T U V W X Y Z

What are these words in code ?

82. POLISH   (_____)

83. SECRET   (_____)

84. TALKING   (_____)

Decode these words.

85. IRKMRI   (_____)

86. EYXLSV   (_____)

A girl was given a packet of sweets which were various colours.
The colours were black, white, yellow, red, green, blue, purple and orange.
There was a different number of each colour and no more than 8 of any one colour.
There were twice as many white sweets as purple sweets and half as many red sweets as blue sweets. There were more orange sweets than black sweets and 3 more green sweets than purple sweets.
The girl decided to eat all the black and green sweets and that would have left 27. However she changed her mind and ate all the black and yellow ones instead and had 23 left.

How many sweets of each colour did she start with ?

87. BLACK   (_____)

88. WHITE   (_____)

89. YELLOW   (_____)

90. RED   (_____)

91. GREEN   (_____)

92. BLUE   (_____)

93. PURPLE   (_____)

94. ORANGE   (_____)